my hungry little

Name :

....

Date of Birth :

....

Age :

....

LITTLE
LUNA PRESS

My
BABY'S
FIRST FOODS
LOG BOOK

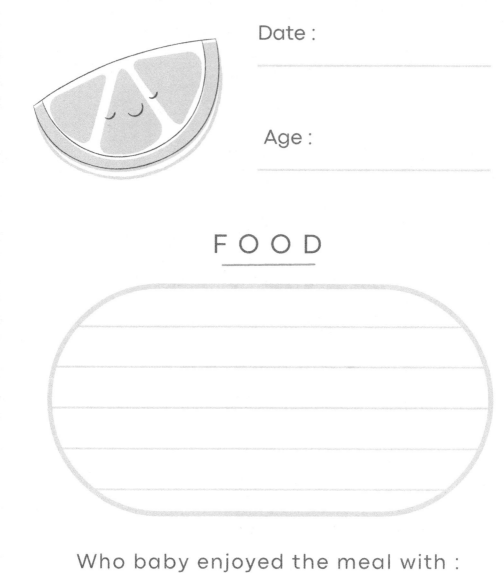

Date :

_____

Age :

_____

F O O D

Who baby enjoyed the meal with :

_____

Spoon
Fed ◯

Hands ◯

Spoon
/ Fork ◯

Baby's Reaction

How food was prepared :

_____
_____
_____
_____
_____

Other notes / tips / things to remember :

_____
_____
_____
_____
_____

Date :

Age :

F O O D

Who baby enjoyed the meal with :

Spoon
Fed ◯

Hands ◯

Spoon
/ Fork ◯

Baby's Reaction

How food was prepared :

_____

_____

_____

_____

Other notes / tips / things to remember :

_____

_____

_____

_____

Date :

Age :

F O O D

Who baby enjoyed the meal with :

Spoon
Fed

Hands

Spoon
/ Fork

Baby's Reaction

How food was prepared :

Other notes / tips / things to remember :

Date :

Age :

F O O D

Who baby enjoyed the meal with :

Spoon
Fed

Hands

Spoon
/ Fork

Baby's Reaction

How food was prepared :

Other notes / tips / things to remember :

Date :

Age :

F O O D

Who baby enjoyed the meal with :

Spoon
Fed

Hands

Spoon
/ Fork

Baby's Reaction

How food was prepared :

_____
_____
_____
_____
_____

Other notes / tips / things to remember :

_____
_____
_____
_____
_____

Date :

Age :

F O O D

Who baby enjoyed the meal with :

Spoon Fed ◯   Hands ◯   Spoon / Fork ◯

Baby's Reaction

How food was prepared :

Other notes / tips / things to remember :

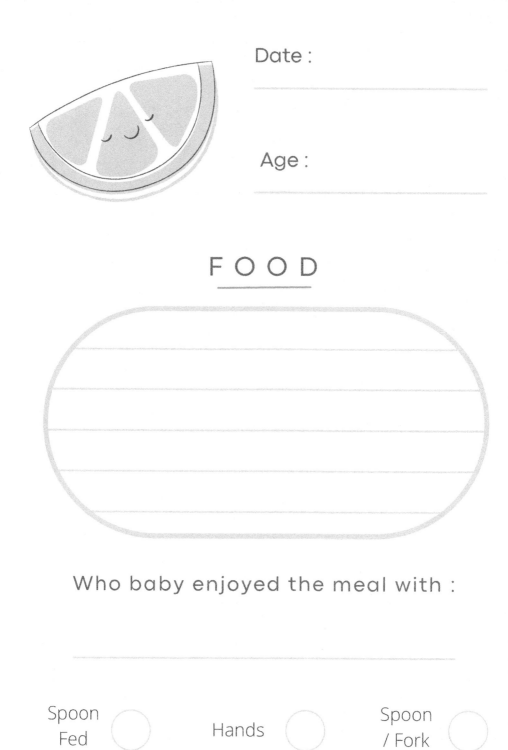

Date :

Age :

F O O D

Who baby enjoyed the meal with :

Spoon
Fed

Hands

Spoon
/ Fork

Baby's Reaction

How food was prepared :

Other notes / tips / things to remember :

Date :

Age :

F O O D

Who baby enjoyed the meal with :

Spoon
Fed

Hands

Spoon
/ Fork

Baby's Reaction

How food was prepared :

Other notes / tips / things to remember :

Date :

Age :

F O O D

Who baby enjoyed the meal with :

Spoon
Fed

Hands

Spoon
/ Fork

Baby's Reaction

How food was prepared :

_____

_____

_____

_____

Other notes / tips / things to remember :

_____

_____

_____

_____

Date :

Age :

F O O D

Who baby enjoyed the meal with :

Spoon
Fed

Hands

Spoon
/ Fork

Baby's Reaction

How food was prepared :

Other notes / tips / things to remember :

Date :

Age :

F O O D

Who baby enjoyed the meal with :

Spoon
Fed ◯

Hands ◯

Spoon
/ Fork ◯

Baby's Reaction

How food was prepared :

_____
_____
_____
_____
_____

Other notes / tips / things to remember :

_____
_____
_____
_____
_____

Date :

Age :

F O O D

Who baby enjoyed the meal with :

Spoon
Fed

Hands

Spoon
/ Fork

Baby's Reaction

How food was prepared :

_____
_____
_____
_____
_____

Other notes / tips / things to remember :

_____
_____
_____
_____
_____

Date :

_____

Age :

_____

F O O D

Who baby enjoyed the meal with :

_____

Spoon
Fed ◯

Hands ◯

Spoon
/ Fork ◯

Baby's Reaction

How food was prepared :

_____
_____
_____
_____
_____

Other notes / tips / things to remember :

_____
_____
_____
_____
_____

Date :

Age :

F O O D

Who baby enjoyed the meal with :

Spoon
Fed ◯

Hands ◯

Spoon
/ Fork ◯

Baby's Reaction

How food was prepared :

Other notes / tips / things to remember :

Date :

_____

Age :

_____

F O O D

Who baby enjoyed the meal with :

_____

Spoon
Fed ◯

Hands ◯

Spoon
/ Fork ◯

Baby's Reaction

How food was prepared :

_____

_____

_____

_____

_____

Other notes / tips / things to remember :

_____

_____

_____

_____

_____

Date :

Age :

F O O D

Who baby enjoyed the meal with :

Spoon Fed Hands Spoon / Fork

Baby's Reaction

How food was prepared :

_____

_____

_____

_____

_____

Other notes / tips / things to remember :

_____

_____

_____

_____

Date :

Age :

F O O D

Who baby enjoyed the meal with :

Spoon
Fed

Hands

Spoon
/ Fork

Baby's Reaction

How food was prepared :

_____
_____
_____
_____
_____

Other notes / tips / things to remember :

_____
_____
_____
_____
_____

Date :

Age :

F O O D

Who baby enjoyed the meal with :

Spoon
Fed

Hands

Spoon
/ Fork

Baby's Reaction

How food was prepared :

Other notes / tips / things to remember :

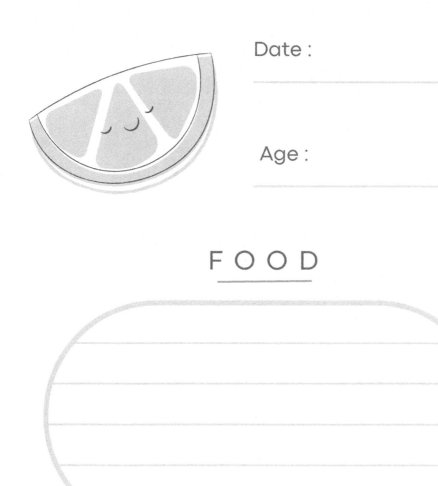

Date : _____

Age : _____

F O O D

Who baby enjoyed the meal with :

_____

Spoon
Fed

Hands

Spoon
/ Fork ◯

Baby's Reaction

How food was prepared :

Other notes / tips / things to remember :

Date :

Age :

F O O D

Who baby enjoyed the meal with :

Spoon
Fed

Hands

Spoon
/ Fork

Baby's Reaction

How food was prepared :

Other notes / tips / things to remember :

Date :

Age :

F O O D

Who baby enjoyed the meal with :

Spoon
Fed

Hands

Spoon
/ Fork

Baby's Reaction

How food was prepared :

_____
_____
_____
_____

Other notes / tips / things to remember :

_____
_____
_____
_____

Date :

Age :

F O O D

Who baby enjoyed the meal with :

Spoon
Fed

Hands

Spoon
/ Fork

Baby's Reaction

How food was prepared :

_____
_____
_____
_____
_____

Other notes / tips / things to remember :

_____
_____
_____
_____
_____

Date :

Age :

F O O D

Who baby enjoyed the meal with :

Spoon Fed ◯   Hands ◯   Spoon / Fork ◯

Baby's Reaction

How food was prepared :

_____

_____

_____

_____

_____

Other notes / tips / things to remember :

_____

_____

_____

_____

_____

Date :

Age :

F O O D

Who baby enjoyed the meal with :

Spoon Fed ◯   Hands ◯   Spoon / Fork ◯

Baby's Reaction

How food was prepared :

_____
_____
_____
_____
_____

Other notes / tips / things to remember :

_____
_____
_____
_____
_____

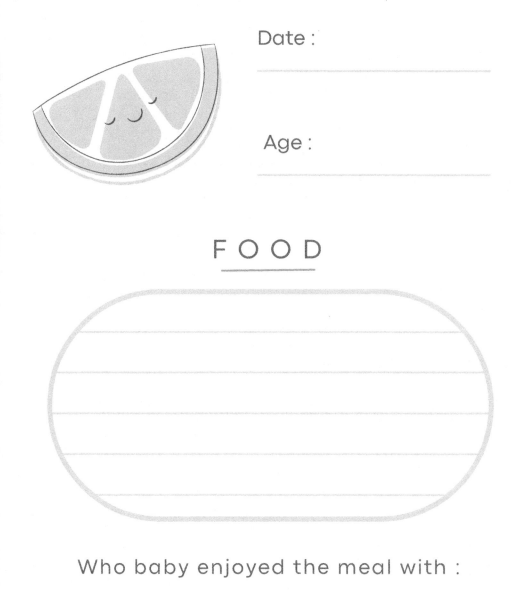

Date :

Age :

F O O D

Who baby enjoyed the meal with :

Spoon
Fed

Hands

Spoon
/ Fork

Baby's Reaction

How food was prepared :

_____
_____
_____
_____
_____

Other notes / tips / things to remember :

_____
_____
_____
_____
_____

Date :

Age :

F O O D

Who baby enjoyed the meal with :

Spoon
Fed ◯

Hands ◯

Spoon
/ Fork ◯

Baby's Reaction

How food was prepared :

_____

_____

_____

_____

Other notes / tips / things to remember :

_____

_____

_____

_____

Date :

Age :

F O O D

Who baby enjoyed the meal with :

Spoon Fed ◯

Hands ◯

Spoon / Fork ◯

Baby's Reaction

How food was prepared :

_____

_____

_____

_____

Other notes / tips / things to remember :

_____

_____

_____

_____

Date :

Age :

F O O D

Who baby enjoyed the meal with :

Spoon
Fed

Hands

Spoon
/ Fork

Baby's Reaction

How food was prepared :

Other notes / tips / things to remember :

Date :

Age :

F O O D

Who baby enjoyed the meal with :

Spoon
Fed ◯

Hands ◯

Spoon
/ Fork ◯

Baby's Reaction

How food was prepared :

Other notes / tips / things to remember :

Date :

Age :

F O O D

Who baby enjoyed the meal with :

Spoon
Fed ○

Hands ○

Spoon
/ Fork ○

Baby's Reaction

How food was prepared :

_____
_____
_____
_____
_____

Other notes / tips / things to remember :

_____
_____
_____
_____
_____

Date :

Age :

F O O D

Who baby enjoyed the meal with :

Spoon
Fed

Hands

Spoon
/ Fork

Baby's Reaction

How food was prepared :

_____
_____
_____
_____
_____

Other notes / tips / things to remember :

_____
_____
_____
_____
_____

Date :

Age :

F O O D

Who baby enjoyed the meal with :

Spoon
Fed

Hands

Spoon
/ Fork

Baby's Reaction

How food was prepared :

_____

_____

_____

_____

_____

Other notes / tips / things to remember :

_____

_____

_____

_____

_____

Date :

Age :

F O O D

Who baby enjoyed the meal with :

Spoon
Fed

Hands

Spoon
/ Fork

Baby's Reaction

How food was prepared :

Other notes / tips / things to remember :

Date :

_____

Age :

_____

F O O D

Who baby enjoyed the meal with :

_____

Spoon
Fed   Hands   Spoon
/ Fork

Baby's Reaction

How food was prepared :

Other notes / tips / things to remember :

Date :

Age :

F O O D

Who baby enjoyed the meal with :

Spoon
Fed

Hands

Spoon
/ Fork

Baby's Reaction

How food was prepared :

_____
_____
_____
_____
_____

Other notes / tips / things to remember :

_____
_____
_____
_____
_____

Date :

Age :

F O O D

Who baby enjoyed the meal with :

Spoon
Fed

Hands

Spoon
/ Fork

Baby's Reaction

How food was prepared :

_____

Other notes / tips / things to remember :

_____

Date :

_____

Age :

_____

F O O D

Who baby enjoyed the meal with :

_____

Spoon
Fed

Hands

Spoon
/ Fork

Baby's Reaction

How food was prepared :

Other notes / tips / things to remember :

Date :

Age :

F O O D

Who baby enjoyed the meal with :

Spoon
Fed ○

Hands ○

Spoon
/ Fork ○

Baby's Reaction

How food was prepared :

Other notes / tips / things to remember :

Date :

Age :

F O O D

Who baby enjoyed the meal with :

Spoon
Fed

Hands

Spoon
/ Fork

Baby's Reaction

How food was prepared :

Other notes / tips / things to remember :

Date :

Age :

F O O D

Who baby enjoyed the meal with :

Spoon
Fed

Hands

Spoon
/ Fork

Baby's Reaction

How food was prepared :

Other notes / tips / things to remember :

Date :

Age :

F O O D

Who baby enjoyed the meal with :

Spoon
Fed

Hands

Spoon
/ Fork

Baby's Reaction

How food was prepared :

Other notes / tips / things to remember :

Date :

Age :

F O O D

Who baby enjoyed the meal with :

Spoon
Fed ○   Hands ○   Spoon
/ Fork ○

Baby's Reaction

How food was prepared :

Other notes / tips / things to remember :

Date :

Age :

F O O D

Who baby enjoyed the meal with :

Spoon
Fed ◯

Hands ◯

Spoon
/ Fork ◯

Baby's Reaction

How food was prepared :

_____

_____

_____

_____

_____

Other notes / tips / things to remember :

_____

_____

_____

_____

_____

Date :

Age :

F O O D

Who baby enjoyed the meal with :

Spoon
Fed

Hands

Spoon
/ Fork

Baby's Reaction

How food was prepared :

Other notes / tips / things to remember :

Date :

Age :

F O O D

Who baby enjoyed the meal with :

Spoon
Fed

Hands

Spoon
/ Fork

Baby's Reaction

How food was prepared :

_____
_____
_____
_____
_____

Other notes / tips / things to remember :

_____
_____
_____
_____
_____

Date :

Age :

F O O D

Who baby enjoyed the meal with :

Spoon
Fed

Hands

Spoon
/ Fork

Baby's Reaction

How food was prepared :

Other notes / tips / things to remember :

Date :

Age :

F O O D

Who baby enjoyed the meal with :

Spoon
Fed

Hands

Spoon
/ Fork

Baby's Reaction

How food was prepared :

Other notes / tips / things to remember :

Date :

Age :

F O O D

Who baby enjoyed the meal with :

Spoon
Fed
○

Hands
○

Spoon
/ Fork
○

Baby's Reaction

How food was prepared :

Other notes / tips / things to remember :

Notes

- - - - - - - - - - -

Made in United States
North Haven, CT
06 June 2023

37456976R00055